LOUD DREAMING IN A QUIET ROOM

LOUD DREAMING IN A QUIET ROOM

Betsy Wheeler

The National Poetry Review Press
Aptos, California

The National Poetry Review Press
(an imprint of DHP)
Post Office Box 2080, Aptos, California 95001-2080

Printed in the United States of America
Published in 2012 by The National Poetry Review Press

ISBN 978-1-935716-12-9

Cover artwork by Melinda Stickney-Gibson
"Buddha Pup," 46: x 24" oil on canvas
melindastickneygibson.com

for Meghan

TABLE OF CONTENTS

Last night as I was sleeping,
I dreamt—marvelous error!—
that I had a beehive
here inside my heart.
And the golden bees
were making white combs
and sweet honey
from my old failures.

~Antonio Machado

NON-SONNET FOR THE *YOU*
BEHIND THE BEDROOM DOOR

Dear Reader, when I say *I mean to ravage you*,
I'm generally talking to ice cubes.
When, pleading in a scaly voice, I say *That's so
out-of-doors of you*, I mean I am afraid you will leave me
with my muffler of sea-green foam, my star-shaped
sunglasses. When I tell you that I love my neighbor,
I actually mean my next-door neighbor—how his crying
makes the trees bow over the house,
makes the grass try to stand up straighter.

When, signed off and halfway sleeping, I murmur
O fabulous coverlet! it means I feel ready for death's comfort.
When I say again *I'll be sorry when this ends*, and my voice
is shards of ice, then I'm not addressing my drink,
but rather the whole mad collection of You.

DAY SAIL WITH DENTAL APPRECIATION

The sky I tuck like a cold garage key
into my little breast pockets.
The water like interference
or a vehicle to grace.
There is no one here.
Peter Björk, you are my
umlaut. I poke and tear you
about my wrangled heart
while your evil wool socks
seek a sort of nirvana.
Peter Björk, the tiniest man
lives inside you. He wears
blue deck shoes. Peter Björk,
I see you there beyond the jib,
leaning railless and quantified.
Your backside is luscious, methinks.
Look there, in the fourth wave starboard:
the beast is grinning through the foam.

WHAT'S BEEN SAID ABOUT WORMHOLES

I woke up speaking,
asking the genius saints of my sleep
to bring me a traveling companion
with loaded eyes. This sounds
like a joke. But believing it is funnier,
and yesterday was better. Let's go there.
What's already happened—
your midnight dancing,
sore chaturanga elbows, the wind
whipping her long hair
like cattails—all become
breadcrumbs for
the long trip back.
Something this good, this beyond
the realm of possibility
should be called gleaming.
When we step out onto the
dark road, its tubular wake,
onlookers will call the noise
we make static—I will call it
loud dreaming in a quiet room.

NON-SONNET FOR A DRYING MOON

Last night, while sleeping, I bent everything I own
in half—woke up sandwiched in my bed and tried
to read the alarm clock's pile of glowing language.

What would Martha do to a room bent all in half?
She's unavailable for comment now, it's true,
but do you also tell the truth only half of the time?

In the middle of every week and once on Sunday,
gardeners work over the entirety of my neighbor's back yard.
It's pretty loud. They have a hot tub they never use.

I would use it. I could use a lot of things. I could use,
for instance, the piece of paper that notes
how many times today you thought of me.

I've been sitting in my cardboard office all day. You don't know
the half of it. And now the late afternoon light in all its warmly
cantankerous glow. I almost forgot to mention the leaves,

tinged as they are now with tangerine. Can you see them?

NON-SONNET FOR ORANGES IN WINTER
AND PEARS, PEARS, PEARS

Waking to Noon spread all over the lawn,
its eyes glazed-over while softly it hums *Silver*
Bells, Silver Bells, and already I cradle
tomorrow in my mouth. All along Main Street,
cloth speakers ring *O Come, O Come,*
O Come all Ye until nightfall finally comes.

I'm still waiting for a power chord, a Russian bard,
the triumphant return of lost marbles. Shooters. Cat's-eyes.

Cat's-eyes: the deepest sphere to look to, hardest
to look at, they look back at you, too true, saying
it was always you you you you. And what now to do.
Bend down to *faithful.* Sidle over to *soon.*
Believe in the fuss that could spell the bell-ringer.
Believe in a noon that could bury me.

FOR INSTANCE, YOUR LIPS

It might be plenty to say *so red*.
But I've never been good
with compliments; that is to say
giving or receiving. I hope that won't
end poorly this drive we've taken
in your parents' car.
Probably I'll keep quiet. Recording the sun
and the leaves and the hills and the sun
and my hand out the window.
Reckless. Restless.

How old are we? That wasn't
animosity. I love your lips.
We had a dream and in it
were banisters floating and plenty
of young people leaning.
The beautiful leaning of dreams came
with us to the edge of this actual bluff where
we fed water to the sparrows in gorgeous
silver ladles. Also lemon pie. Do you
remember it the same way I do?
Funny what we remember of what
we invent in sleeping. Especially
together. So, about your lips—
it was Sunday and the sea was so green.

NON-SONNET FOR TRAIPSING AROUND

The path starts wherever.
Every time I open my eyes I see.

Darkness bends around my wrists, so I
count the tones ringing in my ears or bird cries.
At night, I wrap my arms around my head and

wrangle verbs to save the prairie dogs out there.
This trail I've set myself on—I couldn't.

I wonder about the length of the family vein.
My cousin has a Wurlitzer.

These arms. I have flashing points
of light in the corners of my eyes.
I have so much love for whomever.

COTTAGE RELIC II

A little fleck of night caught in his eye.

The burro in the film stepped and startled, backing away inside the frame.

Charlie Horses whinnied around in back streets buried in the sound of children.

Thick blue chalk left a light dusting on his fingertips.

He bought a painting; in it yellow houses stacked like book spines or teabags.

There was a little bit of night smeared in the frame.

Outside, the same bird in the same tree.

We'll just have to wait, he thought, until the snow melts —children's voices leading him out to the veranda and then back in again.

It isn't chalk, he muttered, it isn't chalk.

The car alarm coming from under the railroad bridge three blocks away could have been a little more specific.

Back streets around his cottage darken down with moonlight.

Spring or a touch of spring, too early to say, he told the bird.

That one small freckle below his lower lip speaks in
Thai.

His favorite frame was just moments from now.
So he waited.

He wanted to let the bird in, feed it a little handful
of grain.

That night still caught in his eye.

His house, his bird, his long white cane.

He could hear the sinking temperature of the rains.

When the film ends—a little flapping sound.
The reel spins.

He cooks French toast with a little nutmeg,
maple-cured bacon.

The slightest bit of night.

In the coming days the bird will just let herself in.

Nights in cooling bathwater.

In through the window to candlelight or moonlight.

A bowl full.

The rain, cold, hangs longer on the branches.

Summer rain is sluttier.

His movement in the bath is deep and conscious.

Children's laughter echoes on long gravel driveways.

Fingers soaked to pruning proves it isn't chalk.

He dries his hands first, water trains down his back.

A bird flew right at the window, but steered course just in time.

The train is almost insignificant, so very few are its cars.

Whistle and bell; it must be morning, the comfort of the steel wheels right on track.

Rain, a little grain, the tiniest beak.

A drawing in blue chalk getting smeared now by the rain.

He says softly to no one her name.

TOURS EVERY HOUR UPON THE HOUR

The gilt-framed painting of a forest
cottage has a soul worthy of frescos.
The hole in the south siding is a square
window into which if you look a view
unfolds a tiny living room and through
that room a door to an even smaller room
whose floors are made of music.

There dances a tiny, bearded goat.
In his eyes blue daisies. Pick one
and you will dance, fool, dance, but not
the dance of the reveling. The petals
of his blues are made for painting
and this is your only way out.

Your first few strokes unveil
a headless halo, a heart bowled
in a pair of hands. The low cello
of Brahms wraps your ankles like
lake weeds and now the roof is peeling off
above you. Around you the frame
cracking its golden square and the world—
O the shine of it!

UNAUTHORIZED BIOGRAPHY
OF CHRISTOPHER SHOLES

The inventor of the typewriter was not by trade an inventor.

A mewing pack of kittens born in his family's barn. Also a duck, but in the pond. A baby in the room painted blue. In his head, a small idea about salmon.

Near to there, a series of explosions; chrysanthemums blooming low in clear skies over Baltimore.

The memory of February was to him fourteen snowballs stored in the icebox.

He could have been 18 or 19, a dead-ringer for Horace.

He went to bed early, thinking of "g" sitting next to "h" or of the closeness that "buttes" holds to "butter."

School and work are sisters, he thought.

He'd wanted out of the family.

As a printer, he was mindful but redundant.

Supper at the library was only allowed in summertime.

Librarian Dan is a "shussher from Shusshville," he pouted.

Migration, though not usually used to describe human travel, appealed to him as a method.

A short report on Wisconsin mining history revealed to him for the first time the food called "pasty" wrapped handily in napkins, then placed in squeaking lunch pails.

His personality was often borderline Collie.

First came the faint rustling of horsemen from under the bedclothes. They probably were hollering "writing machinery!" but what he heard was "riding to Tuileries!" and this would set him back years.

His way of spinning pencils between his thin fingers should have been patented.

That was a very serious idea.

The inflatable jackets were issued to all the riders on the ferry, but he was in the loo.

It was June 23, 1868, and he was very far from home.

SWIMMING UNDERGROUND, I FLOAT FACE UP THINKING OF RAILROADS

This is the logic of a sea-bottom dweller.

This that old practice of wanting; the sound of a horsefly leashed to habit, his green eyes unblinking.

This mind-stable is not fit for children.

This was a station.

This crater-lake hooded with darkness.

This under rock, under soil, under sand, worms, grass, trees, sky, under the clouds and then the stars.

This ground is black water-echoes.

That railing keeps the peepers at a distance.

That road to the surface could slick me away.

This here the temptation.

This plotting best left to the fugitives.

Their absence slaves after their ghostliness: silent, man-shaped holes.

In this moment I wish you were here.

This hidden spot.

The lake is fed, as are we.

And in this way are we aided in reaching.

This next pool—shallow and young.

I fear the station abandoned.

The builders believed in their footing; the solid rock
overhead uncertain but trusted.

This would be the start of their journey.

GOODBYE, RADIO GIRL

Your pink sweater—how it fits. Your questions—
their wings and their whys. All of this is remarkable
but what we remember most is the way
your eyes went there and there. Your questions
and the bees. Those bees acting like ladies on lunch.
Lucky bees and your questions are numerous.
How about that microphone.
Here is an answer held to my chest. Now back to you.
I have an open can but I'm not afraid to hold it.
How about all this sunshine— it makes your sweater
seem all candyish and lamby.
Eyes up here, Radio Girl.
Don't leave us yet with your going there and over there.
The most memorable part was the sheer number of all of you
out there and your fluttering hands.
How many of us there are. Next question.
Her sunglasses are a reflection of your faces
in the crowd, her highlights, yes.
Come here a moment and mind the steps up.
It's like a moving picture but everybody's smoking and nobody's
      eating.
Laughter, sure, but mostly the lower registers: mammalian.
How'd those bees find us again, I'm sorry what did you say?
The answer to that is "sometimes" but I wish it was "never"
      or "always when they open the snack coffin."
I've forgotten my name but I know my place.
Your earlobes, Radio Girl, they seem important.
Or is it your mouth. Your pink sweater.
The way you fit here in floral.
This is the way of the tribes.
The bees and how they swarmed was the answer.

COTTAGE RELIC I

On the mantel, a stuffed grey horse with apparent
   stitches sits.
But that is not enough: it is midnight.

Wild animals gallop wildly in the painting. Their hooves
pounding out a resolution, a heavy touch from gravity.

I am a little sheet-thrasher but nothing
will scare that flock of birds from my sill.

Geese and gravity. Feathers whooshing beneath the
   moon and still
the stream flowing under the stone bridge must shudder
   over the pebbles.

The stuffed gray mantel or stuffing on the mantle.
Apparent stitches.

A rain cloud suspended from the ceiling by only the
   thrumming of a piano chord.

Am I asleep.
Are you asleep.

Geese, gravity, the moon.
How do you fly in your dreams?

All around the house, tree bark the only certainty.
The science of sleep or the science of gravity. The art

of the line.

I want gravity to be a certainty—I fall from my bed just to
    prove it.
Sickness is a Science: for instance, I go out to sea and there
    a little sickness finds me.

In the boat is a forest and in the boat is you and I am in the boat
    and all around
us is water. Floating is a science.

If then over us flies your cousin wearing a red zebra costume,
    we have left
the science of flotation and then we are studying the science
    of sleep.

Or we aren't. Or we sit inside that uncertainty and we write
    a brief letter
and then I reach to steal your pen from around the trunk
    of a not-yet-flowering tree.

The moment we touch it is daytime and no geese are flying
    and the moon
is gone and the world feels heavy again.

Our mantel needs dusting and the mist outside is rain lightly
    icing because it's cold the
Magnolia which will, I promise you in the name of science,
    bloom.

NON-SONNET COMMISSIONING
AN AMBER LOCKET

Oval drop of wretched amber, I curse
your sappy qualities. You're so saving.
So sassy in your slow decline down tree bark.
Poor scorpion. Poor mite. You pour over
their edges and keep. You scallywag the eight-
legged. You bear repeating.

Could you do me for? Could you
syrup my heart in its current,
only mildly-bruised, state? Do a little
save-for-later strung on silver
for a future someone. Best it's done before
more damage comes.

Preserved before the death of it could
case the barely beating.

LOVE LETTER WRITTEN OVER WATER

Dear Unknown Sailor,
Beside the white dawning
of our correspondence I wish
to sit and watch with wonder
the sky unfold. Accompanied
by my little cat, Sancho,
I've taken to sitting at the red
dock's edge—my parasol's
pole lodged in a knothole.
We hear the Muskies growling
below the dock's wide wooden slats,
trolling their long silver bodies
through the lake weeds.
Sancho doesn't scare.
I imagine the fishes' rows
of sharp white teeth are what
is clinking the metal dock poles—
a sound like hollow piano keys or
bone tapping bone.
Tonight, the loons will lilt
their love calls across the lake,
but now, my god or sailboat captain,
the music is machinelike.
Those are those
plucky white jet skis—
various and skyful.

NON-SONNET FOR A NIGHT SAIL

Only in the fourteenth quadrant
of a kaleidoscope belonging to the Sea
Captain's rabbit, may the vanquished portions
of our wanting float without shyness.

Around the Sea Captain's heart flows
a moat that's built for gazing. Come gazing.
Come graze on the memories of strangers,
or gaze at burly knuckles while you feel

your places in need of kneading. Desperate
sailors on the brink of marrying brine will
dance boleros, name names, risk eyeteeth,
do anything to preserve the memory of solid ground.

Or nothing. Everything is what we want.
And so Mars becomes an issue. I'm gazing
at it now—counting its earnest pockets,
bearing its brutal red.

NON-SONNET FOR THE ARTIFACT

I woke up dreaming about headscarves.
Salty climates. In that pileated moment,
you were there and fond of some kind of feather.

Does your mother know? Does she
shake her head, picking at her cuticles—
the frilled layers altogether maternal?

I asked the question again, this time
in a trolley car—orange light purling
through dirty windows, the brass

railings smudged and important. A man's
profile etched on the gray window.
What could he gain from this invented ride?

What is more important involves my navel
and your ear pressed to it. Tell me what you
hear in there, coming from where I came from.

THE VOICE IN THE SKY.

A detonating effect.

The Embassy green and marbleish.

The water below and the bells.

The bells and their salty confidence.

The ruddy lights and we are frozen.

The French had concerns over architecture but others
believed more in signage.

The Ways.

The ways of banners and this flag sewn quietly in that
material is a brooding reminder of borders.

Bilingual schools and plaid skirts four finger-widths
above the knee.

The night. The next city. Stop.

The ground is moving or is it the trees.

Choosing the yellow hairpin is only the beginning
of Wednesday.

The bells, the bells, their clippage.

I have a fiery interior and the damp wind is regretful in that way.

Let's get out of the wind.

For example, let's run for that train about to leave the station.

Something will remain.

That flower, for instance, can have my chair.

Bring your vowels, so adorable in their longness.

How do you hold them like that, just a little bit out from your mouth.

I want to sit inside them.

Talk to me like that.

Reminisce or take the city like that driver took the road.

The train is waiting. The whistle. Bells and bells.

Somewhere in Canada sits a small and blonde historian.

Take her on the road and don't let her go.

Behind us will be any number of possible combinations of the following: percentages, recessions, lack of jobs, brief leases, and vacancy rates.

Their transience is what we love about them.

Touch lightly and go on. Touch it and leave.

The next. The next. Stop.

The voice in the sky, bilingual, says take it and go.

Remember what you forgot.

Keep going.

That voice has a duty but you don't need to know about it.

It's not a secret, right.

The night, the ways and the greenish structure.

The bells and the bells.

That signage.

Reminders of boundaries.

The train. Stop.

MOON STEADY

In this sideshow that features an eyeless catfish,
I will perform an act of creation. Into your cupped

palms I will deposit two parts scentless air and one
part dust. You will feel nothing. In front of your closed

eyes I will produce an invisible, silent moth. Believe me,
I speak from the shadowed wings of stage right, and know

well the ways of deception. I am not keen to that sort
of rubbish. This sideshow act will stand on its own,

it will cherish the life of the eyeless catfish that guards
its one cold gate. The handsome exoskeleton will take

your nickel into her handsome half-shell mouth
and stack it in the pile labeled "alms." You must watch

where your tender settles. You must wear these safety-
goggles and muffle all of your belches. There will be

a closing act that you will wait for and love with a cautious
terror. Now I will float to the middle of a lake that may look

to you like a simple lot of gravel. Don't let my eyes play
tricks on you; I won't even break the surface. I will juggle

these ten bowling pins that spin great figure eights
in a universe parallel to ours. Over there (where? *where?*)

the one-man-show will be missing its one man.
I will now fake my way into art school. I will make

the claim that art is fake, sip iced coffee through a straw,
and comment on everyone's work. I will invoke the spirit

of a stolen yellow bicycle. I will dub myself Ruler of Gerbils.
I will be a new come Muad'Dib. I shall write 8,000 commandments:

There must be spirit in your
                              wanting. When you leave, there
must be something forgiven.

There must be a need-it-now.
There must be a late bus.
There must be odds.

Where there was a blue pickup
                              spotted with rust, there must now be
an owner for a cow labeled "Fence Jumper."

There must be arrangements.
                              There may be a foreskin.
There must be a caught-in-the-rain.

Before you age there must be an ecstasy from
sun-steady to sundown
to moon-up to moon-steady.

There must be talking to the moon and listening
                              for a reply. There must be covalent bonds
and a formula for exactly one kind of pleasure.

There must be introductions
remembered
by those not introduced.

There must be sweat from god-knows-where. There must be
    three-quarter length sleeves.
There must be sweatbands.
There must be hair that is trimmed and hair left well enough
    alone.

There must be thirsty and there
must be salt. There must be
untouchable relics of porcelain.

There must be eggs. There must be dying.
There must be eggs that live. There must be someone to decide.
There must be some way
                              to close the act.

LETTER TO THE SPACE ABOVE

Dear Trouble, I miss you and your
white heels at garden parties, your doilies
playing napkin for blue or red berries.
Your rock-balance. Your hotness.
You are the inch below water, toddlers
and tree bark, the shrieking of girls
in doorways. I covet you, green silk dress,
thin glass stem between fingers. Gazer
at your nurse's ankles, the youngest of your
older students, I'm so into you. Come home,
Rabble Rouser, to these thimbles full of blood.

MY PAST, MY SILVER CANARY

Dear and flowing air above
the river, I am enchanted.
But how would you know
that, stranded three countries
away, chewing on salt.
I dressed myself up
in the red silk you sent
as your love.

Yes, my quarters are kindly,
but the willow
shading the house has
forbidden me callers.
So, I sit window side—
practicing my seventh
posture, dreaming the forest,
hoping for shimmer or a sailor
bearing twelve brands of lace.

DITTY

Hopped-up sax, slowly turning
fan blades, constellations stamped
on the wide belts of the young—
teach me the methods of cool.
I said, capital "C". Because my
heart is too racing. Practically
winning, but not sure of where
it's going. Hands shaking.
Carol says *Right on!* and
I take that to mean keeping.
On. Writing. When she speaks,
there's a wreath of lovely
about her. It's that I mean
being. Her husband's wrists tap-
tapping. And in the streets
not bopping but swinging and
the lampposts, the trees, always ending.

NON-SONNET FOR THE STORM

Rain enough to wash our hair in.
Taxis rush and rush. Cool sirens
trill through the air's sharp wires.
O buckle of brief lightening,
give me some heat to sleep inside.

This riot happening, these twitching eyes.
Marble-mouthed monkeys
shake the trees. Where oh where
will my little house go?
Quick, this door needs barring—
help me whale in the deep.

SOMETHING FOR THE LOW END

Dear Alto Section, you angel me.
Or, I turn in my wings and fall.
You are the afternoon afternoon
curled up in. You workboot
the dangling measures. You speak
in money and money goes south.
You backbone the tenors.
You give me stead.

* * *

If you were naked, you'd be drawn
by a steady hand. If you cared a whit
about callback, you'd saunter in late.
You are the anti-worry my worries wallow in.
You tallish French harlot, I have no knowledge.

* * *

Your parlor is piles
of poison pillows.

Your blue teardrops pool
on my ledges.

Your shades are so Rodeo.
Roh-day-oh.

You are the philosophy

philosophy jacks off in.

*   *   *

You'd forgive half of Chelsea.
A training-wheel to the virgin evenings,
your trailer's gone begging.
You're so dark-washed.
You look better in Cranberry.
You should take off your sweater.
Take your hands out your pockets.

*   *   *

Life doesn't have to be
this way. It could be
handsomer. It could make
the sound of plastic beads
jumping. It wants to be accordion-
music on your birthday morning.
Never mind what was muted,
it's sort of mysterious. It's incredibly
transparent. It's immune to all public
blunders and subsequent embarrassment.
It's already home in bed by now,
poor thing.

NON-SONNET FOR TELLING YOU EVERYTHING

Like how high banjo trills make me go electric.
Like how charity. Like how gold.
Like I'd like to take you in and feed you a little
sweet milk. Like you'd mind, but I'm so
tired of honesty like California fault lines.
Like how this is the big moment.
Like, now.
Like how cuteness rules the dating quadrants.
Like how sexy. Like when I say you look good
in white linen, I mean sheets. Like I'd like to
rob your booty bank. Like how I'd take my
winnings to the grave.

NON-SONNET FOR FREE SPEECH ZONES

The wire rabbit in the looking-glass past has forgotten
his stuttering sculptor. One side of his face is bare
of whiskers, and thusly he orbits the realm of imagination
and surrealist interpretation. You want to give him food.
I want to bend his ear toward me and spout a theory on
the missing bones of Paleo-Indian I. Those hairy bones
of the catfish. I believe they were abducted by alien
paleontologists digging for dirty handmaiden-clues.

Soon, the rabbit's barbed cohort will arrive and they will bind
themselves together as fences made for catching foxes.
Smart little rabbit, how do you keep from rusting in the rain?
Wafting my hand around your borders, I test the pickled air.
I see the tools of penning and believe you are no cage.

ROBBED AND SWUNG LOW INTO REVERIE

And so the wind, humid but welcome, comes around to rub its faint body against our houses, attaching everyone to everyone else. Nobody is famed for anything; not the hymn-writers, or sous chefs, not the marathoners. All just living or have lived in that particular house of the body.

One body is similar in silhouette to eight other bodies, is opposite in skin texture to six. One body will fit perfectly in bed with nine others, will violently reject seven, and is momentarily indistinguishable from five. Here is where things get tricky.

Some of these bodies will find each other on scooters in the streets of Rome, or weeding in the public gardens of Minneapolis, maybe trespassing the high dunes of North Carolina's coastline. Some of the best-known meetings will become the stuff of hymns. Others, the catalyst for wars. Were it up to me, I would have written one of the odds much higher. Guess which one.

I'd like to say our young bodies fit perfectly, but it's more accurate to say our limbs locked like softly notched gears, our engines wheeling. I was stunned. I mean, stung. I mean, our skin sung brightly on that foreign river. We looked impossible, effortless. A low tide. Love's circuitry unmapped but gently numbered. He was of the eight. Or maybe the nine. O, I believe in believing in the nines.

NON-SONNET FOR SLEEPING BIRDS

Early morning light spills trails
of aqua in its quiet promenade.
I've been here before.

Consciousness, its brutal water wheel,
spins for hours and the morning brings
a hardy slipper I have not called for.

Nights in half-lit rooms, my peripheral vision
catches shadows of running dwarves, black cats
in masquerade, a skunk who preens his plume.

I only look when I'm ready to see.
I think the hallway is breathing.

BUFFALO CHURCH

By and by the sound of women's singing presses its
gentle knees to my ears.

By the river they wanted to lead me.

Past the groundswell; little homes stuffed into hillsides.

The silence between high-notes was scary-scary.

The air terrarium-still, or stuck like jellyfish poison
slowly sewing its way through the ocean's deep breezes.

Pioneers no doubt would have fled.

But look at us standing here, remembering 1773
as a year of great darkness; the foreman all
broken up about something or other, his hands steamy
and sad, brushing away brown rivulets of sweat.

Flung into thirst, we ride through past and present all
at once.

Church me, you say. *Church me the hell out of here.*

And I will.

Replace my heart with stone and I will.

I will fling me, church you, toward that light stands
a mile to the north.

THE QUARRY

Let's go diving in the quarry
where we shouldn't go at night.

Green water lit by cherries and the hum
of purring eels.

I'm already in
way past my toes by now.

A hunger for accordion music
played well, over the din of silent measures.

I say it's melting over me
and it melts over me.

NON-SONNET FOR A RUFFLED BIRD

The weather knows nothing about me at all.
I am regal in the gale, hunkered down,
unaffected by the winch-head's stormy method.
Yeah, I hold myself together pretty well.
I'm all about collecting.
This fire in my palms, for instance, is amazing
in its tender and neurotic burning. I admit
that what I'm afraid of has a higher potency:
the possibility that my body could hurl me,
without asking, over an eighteen-story railing
and would I grapple for a toe-hold? Would the wind,
oblivious and busy anyway, take note and sweep me
back up? I have no comeuppance for the storm,
reactionary or otherwise. I have no nest to build.

Imminent rain, carry me slippery inside
your mother cloud or let me burn in flight.

AFTER THE PARTY,
THERE IS A LONELY SOUND.

Sound of a rowboat knocking emptily
against the dock. Sound of smooth oars banging
loosely against sideboards. Sound of night.
Sound of stars. Sound of blinds zipped down
against the sleeping country. Sound
of lovely. Sound of we're all going home,
what about you? Sound of the thinness
of dimes and the hard snap of butterscotch.
The sound of lapping water makes me want to stay all night long.
Sound of a piano being played upstairs and a small boy's
blanket of sheet music. Sound of the ceiling
as some sort of possibility. Sound
of I'll always write to you. Sound of letters
stolen from mailboxes. Sound of waiting.
Sound of eyes wide open. Sound the cello makes.
Sound of the grass in the yard taking on the dew.
Sound of that's it.
Sound of yes and yes and yes.

NON-SONNET FOR THE PHRASE
"BUT I BELIEVE."

This afternoon slowly flaking away in sheaths.
3:00 grandfathered in. Collector's stamps
accidentally licked and posted, the Basil Dove
heckling the rest of the postal pouch.
Leaves faking change and then the guard.

To the waitress I said wondermeat, meaning
wonderment, meaning I wonder where you are,
and how you spend your wooden nickels.
Every cup of coffee after noon counts as addiction,
but nothing compared to how much I miss you.
Your gleeful, airless laugh. Your lashes lashing.

We are both born and dying in love's mystery.
Penelope weaving and unweaving her weaving.
I say I do not believe. I do not believe.

NON-SONNET FOR INNUMERABLE SUNS

Sometimes in summer heat it's just good to lie here.
Lie in bed. When I do, I think sometimes of you,
stirring your third cup of coffee with a little spoon.

I want to pick up everyone I love from a distance
and place them in the cities that I know.
In a movie we saw once, a man lay dying

in his bed—his right hand resting over his heart.
He tapped his chest with his index finger twice—
was it reassurance or impatience? I don't know.

Tap your chest now, old lover. Assure me of nothing.
Innumerable suns have circled this place and us.
I'm not coming back this time. No matter for your hands.

I have all sorts of hope.

HOW VERY LEWIS AND CLARK OF ME

But for I am a slinky little voyager.

But for I am built like a keelboat: with critical eyes,
a transcontinental gaze.

But for men chase my fame, want my frame in their
king-size.

But for my long ears clouded by white curls.

But for my expedition.

But for baying around slackwater and liftlocks.

But for I reconnoiter the hill peak.

But for the creaking of love trees.

But for I find you I will lay down my arms.

I will lay down my arms and be.

START HERE

Down and down—the lights, the sun.
Pink and white tree petals, teacups
bowled among the leaves. Soft,
the light skin of wrists, the yellow lids
of tulips shaken down to the green
and still rain-soaked lawn.
Down the houselights in the theater—
its golden walls and simulated architecture.
Voices and stardom clinging to the heavy
velvet curtains. The gardenscapes
on the seat upholstery rubbed
shinily away. Down the lights so the strings'
tuning tapers off and the woodwinds
hold their low notes, their loping breath.
Down the lights and tittering whispers
from the box seats—new lovers touching
knee to knee and thinking fingertips on skin.
The conductor raises his arms.

* * * *

Down and down, the rain softly down.
A bus full of travelers moves slowly
along the back roads; through Pennsylvania,
New Jersey, past hand-painted signs
"Vote: NO Quarry, Save Our Land,"

past white-walled diners with neon

soup signs—behind the cook framed

black & whites of passerby celebrities

who tried his Shoofly Pie.

Downriver to the city—not my city.

Down and down.

The shingles, roofs of abandoned

buildings— their blacked-out windows.

Downhill a roller rink, the gravel

of the empty lot. Boys chasing girls

with ropes of cherry licorice, Slurpee kisses,

and who wants a small Tombstone Pepperoni

after they've already eaten? Everyone.

Down and down into the valley,

memories—touching and away again, pushing off.

Moving ever closer to the city,

the lights of the city, those buildings

lit and blinking —

so much better to see by. So much

better to see you. I switch busses

in Lehighton and on down

along the river we go.

*   *   *   *

Darkness in the yards of my childhood

neighborhood ghost   graveyard   shadows

running and whispers something

maybe   a hedge maybe   a collie a small

hay bale   Dark   I'm a serious

child who'd roll seriously down the yard

laughing for all that's serious but come

nighttime   I need night vision   goggles

green on the screen   night vision   ghost

in the graveyard I can

hear you but I can't see

you come out

come out

wherever you are

*   *   *   *

Andrew, my childhood

memories have you in my

sandbox. You cracking

milkpods open for the silk

to brush lightly against

my neck. You and red

clover, honeysuckle, hay.

I pick apart the purple heads

for you to taste—the first sweet

flower for your lovely tongue. You

running with me past birches,

breaking the woodline into a hot

and golden hayfield we are running

just to run.   Now it's you in the pinewoods;

my darkest playforest. The pines

with their low branches are easy

to climb. Sap on my palms,

needles sticking into my pigtails,

curled bark pulling away into my hands.

I climb to show you I can, it's my

tree and see I can do it.   Come

down you say Come back

down here I want to kiss

you on the mouth.

*   *   *   *

Over the bridge, the N

running over the East River.

From his apartment,

the train is toysized but I hear

it running. Sun setting

and to the east the gray steeples

of Park Slope nose up into an evening

haze over Gowanus Canal.

The panes of the warehouses

burn the bright orange of sundown—
building almost on fire. Down the sun,
up the lights and finally a night
without rain. The rooftops
from here seem leapable: tar,
grass, over the stinking canal,
under the sun, leap from here to—
roof to roof never looking down.
Going down and I could fly to the park,
through the sundrone—the treetops
a bright and painful green before going
black and nothing but darkness.

* * * * *

Andrew, there's too much
rain. June here is rain
and you a whole country away,
farther than Paris. Andrew,
I remember your face, lips,
your sleek neck, thin
hips, darling, your tiny
moles. Andrew, keep
your shirt off. Your bare
chest makes me think Paris
is closer and everything

is possible. Your darkness,

so light, come down

here, come up. Come.

Take care of your knees.

Remember my hair draped

over your shoulder.

After you left me

the cabbie said I

smelled like a Jersey girl.

Hairspray and onions.

Whiskey. Sex.

Tell me all

that you remember.

*   *   *   *

Brooklyn, you're so

much better to me.

We should date a little and settle

down—me in you, you're

already in me. Country

Mouse. Not my city but

your plane surfaces,

buildings, tall poets

walking your streets I

love them and you my

second city. Your bagels,

lox, your rusty gates,

pinball bars and too

much scotch. Tobacco.

I'm moved by you.

Moving into you, I'm

coming down forever.

Yes, Brooklyn, I do.

I've fallen. Falling. Love,

come down—

come together. The lights

slowly going down.

Not my life but my sight.

Shrinking aperture.

The curtain's close and

call. That's all, folks.

Down. The lights dim

down and dimmed. Dimming to

nighttime. A balcony and no

railing. Earlier the theater

and then to take the dog out.

Down and down, I will

miss this I mean I think I will

miss him.

*   *   *   *

Once a ballerina,
once a trumpet
player. Once a
woman in a long
evening gown holding
a microphone.
All waited and waiting
behind that curtain.
Obviously once
is a lie it's more like
often but all waited and
counted heard the
crowd hush on cue,
dimming of the lights
means real world is closed
for business, now for
imagination. All the world
dark, attention front and center.
That spot in the middle
sharp, well-lit. What matters
most because that's all there is.
All around has fallen down.
I don't mean the dancer fell,
or the singer tripped and went
down on her exit. What I mean

is when one part of the
world goes dark, there's
another by comparison
illuminated, bright.
What kind of applause
ends a fabulous evening?
When the strings stop
their humming, are they hot?
Does the audience stand
and mean ovation because
the lights are up and let
the dancers see our
happy smiling faces. We thank
you. Please do it again. In this
scene, the lights come back on
and the crowd goes home
with different hungers.

*   *   *   *   *

Brooklyn, I've sat a little in you
like so many others.
Friends around tables and
steam from hot drinks
rise up to all of their
faces. Come over here

and sit by me why don't you
sit by me. Boots with
tall zippers and coffee
with unspillable lids.
Paper bags. Bodegas.
How many languages
do you speak fluently? I'm
easy that way and willing
to work. I can
work pretty hard. I'm
what those magazines
call 'fiercely independent'
and so when years from now I
reach in the darkness for your
elbow at the curb, I will
do the reaching. I love
you don't take
care of me.

*   *   *   *   *

Andrew, this poem
is not for you.
The rain came back today,
long lost and gone and
you away and come back

with poems. Sending love
electronically and this
is not for you. The cicadas
are incessant—
their black and shining
bodies on the front
porch of my neighbor;
solid and lazy, forged and
particular, armored
but easily crushed and
all at once they are
everything and why
did you even come here?
Did you sleep all summer
long outdoors and under
a motherless someone and me
so far from you and your
sending me love poems
to another is not what I
wanted and Andrew this
poem is not for you. It
is me at 5 a.m. waking
to no one and when I
interrupt my own sleep
to stumble to the bathroom
it is blindness and lonely or

lovely and who I am which

is me, which is never

so clear.

It is me writing

myself back into

sleep so I just drink

the water, I just

drink the water and think

something has to

start here.

ACKNOWLEDGEMENTS

Sincerest thanks to the editors of the following magazines, in which many of these poems, or earlier drafts of them, first appeared: *Absent, All Small Caps, Avatar Review, Bat City Review, Bedside Guide to No Tell Motel, Caffeine Destiny, Forklift Ohio, Gut Cult, The Journal, MiPoesias, No Tell Motel, Octopus, Pebble Lake Review, Pindeldyboz, Ping Pong,* and *Prelude,* and to Jen Hyde and Small Anchor Press, who first published the final poem of this collection as the limited-edition chapbook *Start Here.*

The epigraph of this book comes from the poem "Last Night As I Was Sleeping" by Antonio Machado, translated by Robert Bly.

Thanks also to The Ohio State University MFA program, the Juniper Institute at UMass Amherst, and the Stadler Center for Poetry at Bucknell University for offering the space and financial support needed to write these poems.

Especial thanks to the following individuals for their advice (editorial and otherwise) in putting these poems and this book together, and for sharing the life: Dean Gorman, Chad Oness, August Herling, Kathy Fagan, Maggie Smith, Sean Flanigan, Kelly McGuinness, Adam Cole, Rebecca Barry, Cindy King, Dean Young, Matt Rhorer, Joshua Beckman, Lisa Olstein, Dara Wier, and Matthew Zapruder.

My utmost gratitude goes to: C.J. Sage, for ushering this book into the world; to Melinda Stickney-Gibson, for allowing us the use of her painting "Buddha Pup" for the book cover; and to Meghan Dewar, for all else.

Betsy Wheeler completed her MFA in poetry at The Ohio State University. From 2005-2007 she held the Stadler Fellowship at Bucknell University. Her poems have appeared in *Bat City Review*, *The Journal*, *Pebble Lake Review*, *Forklift Ohio*, *Octopus*, and elsewhere. Her chapbook, *Start Here*, was published in 2007 by Small Anchor Press. She is Managing Director for the Juniper Summer Writing Institute at University of Massachusetts Amherst and is editor of Pilot Books—a publisher of limited-edition poetry chapbooks. She lives in Northampton, Massachusetts.

Also from The National Poetry Review Press:

Lucktown by Bryan Penberthy

Bill's Formal Complaint by Dan Kaplan

Gilgamesh at the Bellagio by Karl Elder

Legend of the Recent Past by James Haug

Urchin to Follow by Dorine Jennette

The Kissing Party by Sarah E. Barber

Deepening Groove by Ravi Shankar

The City from Nome by James Grinwis

Fort Gorgeous by Angela Vogel

Please visit our website for more information:

www.NationalPoetryReview.com

CPSIA information can be obtained at www.ICGtesting.com
Printed in the USA
LVOW091504170412

277996LV00007B/10/P